Build a Flower

Build a Flower

A Beginner's Guide to Paper Flowers

Lucia Balcazar

ABRAMS, NEW YORK

Editor: Meredith A. Clark
Designer: Laura Palese
Production Manager: Kathleen Gaffney

Library of Congress Control Number: 2019936963

ISBN: 978-1-4197-4064-0
eISBN: 978-1-68335-881-7

Copyright © 2020 Abrams
Photography by Glenn Scott

Cover © 2020 Abrams

Printed and bound in China

10 9 8 7 6 5 4 3 2 1

Abrams books are available at special discounts when purchased
in quantity for premiums and promotions as well as fundraising
or educational use. Special editions can also be created to
specification. For details, contact specialsales@abramsbooks.com
or the address below.

Abrams® is a registered trademark of Harry N. Abrams, Inc.

ABRAMS The Art of Books
195 Broadway, New York, NY 10007
abramsbooks.com

INTRODUCTION 8

1 Paper Basics 15

2 Tools and Materials 25

3 Care Instructions 31

4 Techniques 35

5 Tutorials for Basic Flowers 63

Cardstock Wall Flower 64

Doublette Crepe Paper Tulip 72

Florist Crepe Paper Open Peony 80

Fine Crepe Paper Butterfly Ranunculus 90

Tissue Paper Dahlia 100

6 Beyond Flowers 109

TEMPLATES 122 / GLOSSARY 124

RESOURCES 126 / ACKNOWLEDGMENTS 128

Welcome to Paper Flowers!

Handcrafted paper flowers are experiencing a **revival**, becoming increasingly popular among contemporary crafters. The **versatility** of paper makes flowers a great project choice for a variety of events, decorations, and **gifts**.

This book is intended to be an introduction to paper crafting through flowers. In it, you will find descriptions of the most popular types of **paper**, as well as **basic tools and materials** and how to use them. You will learn beginner and intermediate **techniques**, such as curling, cupping, and fringing, to add depth and dimension to your paper flowers.

You'll also find **step-by-step instructions** on how to build five paper flowers, with each tutorial exploring a new technique and a different type of paper. You can then add your own **creative** touch with the optional coloring techniques using supplies like acrylics, inks, and pastels. Inspiration can be found in nature for color, texture, and shape, all within one flower. **Apply** your everyday discoveries to your paper flowers and you will be surprised at how **playful** and modern they turn out. After all, we are not looking to perfectly replicate a flower—instead, we are trying to capture each flower's **unique** personality.

Although there are no set rules, the **tips and tricks** in this book will help you get comfortable with the art of paper flower **crafting**. With a little bit of cutting, stretching, and gluing, you will be able to create your own one-of-a-kind, **beautiful** paper flowers.

**BUTTERFLY
RANUNCULUS** *page 90*

PEONY *page 80*

TULIP *page 72*

WALL FLOWER *page 64*

DAHLIA *page 100*

1

PAPER
BASICS

The most important material you will need to make paper flowers is, of course, paper. Different types of paper work better for different flowers. Consider the weight, texture, and color of the flower you want to create as you select the paper you'll use to build it. You can stick to the recommended paper on each tutorial, or try different paper and follow the suggested adjustments at the end of the instructions. As you progress, you will want to experiment with different qualities and types of paper in your flower projects.

Types of Paper

Here are the most common and popular
types of paper used to make paper flowers, as well
as many other paper crafts.

CARDSTOCK PAPER

from 50 lb to 110 lb

Cardstock paper is a thicker version of the regular text-weight paper you find in an office printer. Cardstock is readily available at a number of craft stores and found in a wide variety of colors. It generally comes in 8½-by-11-inch (21.5-by-28-cm) sheets that vary in thickness. Because it's so thick, it's not easy to manipulate into lifelike petals, but it works great for modern and oversize flowers and is perfect for paper flower backdrops that need to be sturdy and durable. Decorating cardstock paper usually requires opaque media, including acrylics and layered paper techniques.

FINE CREPE PAPER

32 g and 60 g

Fine crepe paper is thin and delicate with a smooth finish and a gentle stretch. Its translucency gives petals a lifelike quality that other papers lack. You can color fine crepe with chalk pastels for gradients and use markers for petal edges. For added sturdiness, you can fuse two sheets of fine crepe into a sheet of "doublette" with spray adhesive or fusible bonding web. Fine crepe works great for making flowers with many petals, like the butterfly ranunculus. In a pinch, crepe paper streamers can give you a similar effect to fine crepe paper.

DOUBLETTE CREPE PAPER

90 g

Doublette crepe paper, also known as German crepe paper or double-sided crepe paper, actually refers to two sheets of fine crepe paper fused together, but the result feels completely different from the original material. Doublette paper stretches just the right amount to shape petals and has a smooth texture. The grain is not as noticeable as with heavier crepe, and there are no horizontal machine lines. Doublette paper comes in double-sided folds that measure approximately 10-by-49 inches (25-by-124 cm), and each side has a slightly different color—like bubblegum and rose, or olive green and forest green. When gently wet with a brush, both colors will blend together. You can color doublette paper with alcohol inks, watercolors, and India inks; it absorbs paint beautifully.

FLORIST CREPE PAPER

100 g, 160 g, and 180 g

Florist crepe paper, also known as Italian crepe paper, is thick and textured paper with a fantastic stretch that allows you to create deep, sculptural petals. It is sturdy and will hold its shape well, but most brands have horizontal machine lines every 2 inches (5 cm) that you may want to avoid when cutting your petals. There are some florist crepe paper brands that have no machine lines.

TISSUE PAPER

20 g to 24 g

Tissue paper is widely accessible and often used for gift wrapping—giving you a great way to upcycle your gift-wrapping materials. It does not stretch, but it can be dyed in wonderful shades. In a pinch, coffee filters can give you a similar effect to tissue paper.

OTHER, LESS-COMMON TYPES OF PAPER

Here are some papers that can also work for making flowers, depending on your project: streamer crepe paper, coffee filters, watercolor paper, wrapping paper, kraft paper, decorative paper, text-weight paper, newsprint, book pages, music sheets.

DOUBLETTE CREPE PAPER

FINE CREPE PAPER

FLORIST CREPE PAPER

CARDSTOCK PAPER

TISSUE
PAPER

An Important Note on the Grain of Crepe Paper

When working with crepe paper, you will need to consider the direction of the grain of the paper. The grain of the paper refers to the vertical lines that run up and down your paper roll or fold of paper. These lines give crepe paper its stretchiness. Crepe paper only stretches when you pull it perpendicularly to the grain. When you cut your petals, it is important that your template matches the direction of the grain—otherwise you won't be able to stretch your petal. Keep this in mind when cutting and folding your paper. In this book, dimensions are given as height-by-length, so that the grain of the paper runs with the height of your petal.

TOOLS
AND
MATERIALS

Beyond paper, the basic tools needed to become a paper flower master are very similar to those employed by florists. You will need floral wire, floral tape, and wire cutters—as well as common crafting tools like scissors and glue.

SCISSORS

A good pair of scissors is your most important tool for making paper flowers. There are many types of scissors to choose from, but a standard pair of crafting scissors will suffice. These have long blades and pointy tips, allowing you to both cut large areas and make detailed cuts. Depending on the thickness of the paper and how sharp your scissors are, you may be able to cut many petals at once without the edges getting rough. Other types of scissors you may find useful include fringing scissors, pinking shears, and decorative-edge scissors. Look for ones with soft-grip handles to protect your hands during long periods of cutting.

GLUE

There are three basic types of glue that work best for paper flowers: hot glue gun, tacky glue, and glue stick. A small hot glue gun will create a strong bond and dry quickly. Be sure to use a low temperature setting, and be careful not to burn yourself. Tacky glue is good for precision work. It won't create as much bulk in the stem when attaching the petals, and you'll have more time to reposition petals before the glue has dried. To apply tacky glue, you can use a small brush, a dowel, a glue dispenser, or your fingers. A glue stick is less messy and will also allow you to reposition and laminate petals easily. When choosing a glue stick for flower-making, be sure you're working with extra-strength glue and not the all-purpose school glue.

FLORAL TAPE

Floral tape can be a little tricky for beginners because it works differently than regular tape. The adhesive activates only when you stretch it, and the tape sticks only to itself. As you wrap your wire with floral tape, you must continuously stretch and pull down on the tape with one hand as you twist the wire with your other hand. Depending on your technique, floral tape can be your only type of adhesive, or you can skip the floral tape altogether if you use a good quality glue. I mainly use floral tape as an extra layer of security after I've glued all of my petals. You can also use it to thicken your stem if needed. Floral tape is available in a wide range of colors. The most common ones are dark green, brown, and white. For a more finished look, you can cover your floral tape with strips of stretched-out crepe paper and glue.

FLORAL STEM WIRE

Floral stem wire comes in a variety of thicknesses, measured on a scale of 16 gauge to 32 gauge. The lower the gauge, the thicker the wire. You will find floral wire in three main forms: plain, paper-covered, or cloth-covered. An 18 to 20 gauge plain or cloth-covered wire is good for stems, and 24 to 28 gauge white paper-covered wire is good for wiring petals and leaves. Floral stem wire usually comes in lengths of 18 inches (46 cm). It's easier to work with a smaller wire length when first starting out. If you later need a longer stem, you can always lengthen your stem with another wire and floral tape.

FLORAL STEM WIRE

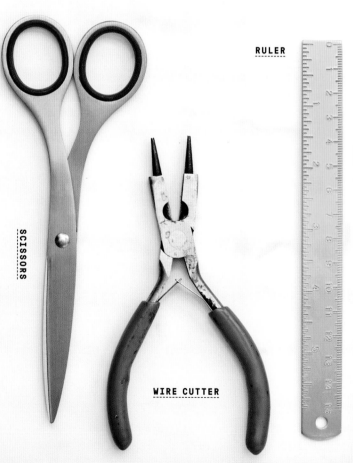

SCISSORS

WIRE CUTTER

RULER

GLUE GUN

VARIETY
OF PAPER

FLORAL TAPE

GLUE

CARE

INSTRUCTIONS

To take care of paper flowers, you have to do the opposite of what you would do with real flowers: keep them away from direct sunlight and water. Below are more detailed tips on how to keep them looking fresh and beautiful for a long time.

LIGHT

Most paper is not completely fade resistant. If left in direct sunlight for prolonged periods of time, its color will fade. You can either keep your paper flowers away from exposure to direct sunlight or protect them with a light-fast method. One that works really well is UV-resistant matte spray. Make sure to spray your flower evenly from a distance of at least 15 inches (38 cm). The colors may darken a bit after treatment, so experiment with sample flowers or scrap paper before spraying your finished flower. Spray in a well-ventilated area.

Another method for protecting your flowers from sunlight is using Mod Podge to seal the color. Use a flat or foam brush to apply a thin layer to your petals and/or leaves. Mod Podge will also thicken and strengthen your flower, but the finish of the petals will change.

Finally, you can cover your flower in wax to protect it from the elements. This is done by holding your flower upside down by the stem, slowly submerging it in a pot of hot wax, removing it, and shaking off excess wax.

WATER AND MOISTURE

Keep in mind that most paper is not waterproof or even water-resistant. The colors will run if wet, and petals will lose their shape. Some types of glue are more resistant to humidity, but in general, most glue will dissolve in high humidity. If you want your paper flowers to last, do your best to keep them dry.

DUST

To protect your flowers from dust, keep them in an enclosed space, such as a bell jar or glass case. To clean your flowers, hold them upside down and tap them gently. You can also lightly blow on them or use a small, clean brush to gently dust them off.

TECHNIQUES

Building a paper flower involves carefully crafting the individual parts of the flower—the center, stamens, petals, calyx, stem, and leaves—using a variety of basic crafting techniques, and then assembling the parts. For a basic flower, you will start by building the center, then surrounding it with stamens and adding the petals either individually, in clusters, or in strips/layers. For a more finished look, you'll next attach the calyx, cover the stem with paper, and add matching leaves.

Paper flower crafting techniques allow you to shape petals and attach them to the stem to make them look more natural and give them movement and dimension. The type of paper you choose will determine the technique you use for shaping the petals. Most types of crepe paper have a decent stretch and can be shaped by cupping and ruffling. But even if the paper has no stretch, there are ways to manipulate it through folding and cutting that will give the petals some dimension. Practice each technique on scrap pieces of paper before attempting them on your actual petals. You can also refer to these techniques when following the tutorials.

Using Templates

You can cut out the parts for your flowers using the templates from this book as guides. Trace the templates onto a white sheet of paper and cut them out. Then draw around these outlines on cardstock and cut out the cardstock shapes. You can also trace your template with pencil directly onto the paper you are using to create your flower. Either way, make sure the template arrows match the direction of the grain. All dimensions in this book are given as height-by-length, and the grain of the paper should be running with height, up and down the longest part of your petal. The dotted lines on the templates are guides to where the paper should fold or gather.

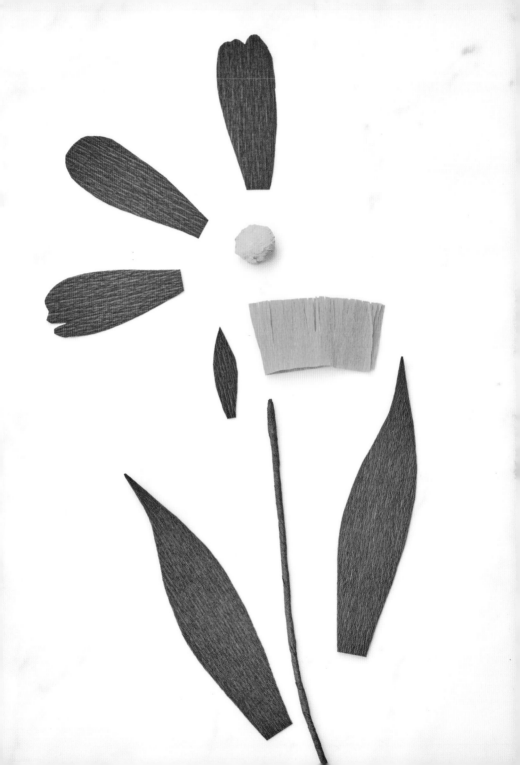

Cutting

To cut out the parts, place your cardstock template on top of your paper and cut around it, or cut out the shapes you traced directly onto the paper. After some practice, you will be able to cut your petal shapes freehand, without a guide. Depending on the sharpness of your scissors, you can cut multiple petals at once by layering pieces of paper on top of each other. I recommend cutting no more than three or four petals at once when using florist crepe, doublette crepe, or cardstock. For thinner papers, like tissue and fine crepe, you can cut up to ten petals at once. To do this, accordion-fold your paper along the grain and place your template on top. You should meet no resistance if you're folding your paper along the grain.

Cupping

Cupping is a technique used to mimic a petal's naturally round shape. You will mostly cup papers that have at least some kind of stretch, like crepe papers. It will take some practice at first, but it will soon become intuitive. To cup, hold the middle of your petal with your thumbs and index fingers and gently stretch it into a subtle bowl shape. As you stretch the paper, move your thumbs toward yourself. Repeat this motion around the petal's surface to get your desired shape. Some flowers, like roses and closed peonies, call for a more pronounced bowl shape and should only be cupped around the middle. Others, like open peonies and magnolias, need a more elongated petal and should be cupped all around the petal. Try not to stretch the edges of the petal or the paper will become flimsy.

Snipping, Scrunching, and Twisting Petal Bases

You can also shape papers that have no stretch, such as cardstock and tissue paper, by manipulating the base of the petal (the bottom part that attaches to the flower's center or stem) to create a slightly cupped or raised petal. Here are techniques for manipulating the petal's base.

Snipping or making a slit at the base of the petal and gluing the two resulting flaps together. The longer the size of your cut and the more you overlap your flaps, the more cupped and raised your petal will be. This technique is especially useful for sturdy papers like cardstock and oversize flowers.

Scrunching the base of your petal. This technique works well with flimsy papers like tissue. It will also keep multiple tissue petals together before they're attached to the stem. Use your fingertips to scrunch the base of your petals for flowers like anemones, roses, and poppies.

Twisting the base of your petal. You can roll the base of your petals between your fingers to create a thinner base and give dimension to your petal. Attaching a petal with a twisted base is easier when you use a hot glue gun.

Curling

Curl your petals to simulate a live petal's natural curve and movement. You can curl the petal edges by wrapping them around a small
rounded tool, like a pencil, paintbrush, or dowel. The intensity of the
curl will depend on how thick or thin your rounded tool is. To curl your
whole petal, you can run it along the edge of your scissors using a
similar movement to that of curling ribbon. Place the petal between
your thumb and the edge of your scissors and pull the petal with
your other hand while pressing your thumb against the scissors.
The more times you do it, the more pronounced the curl will be.
Generally, you will curl your petals after cutting them but before
cupping or ruffling them.

Laminating

Laminating your paper consists of gluing two pieces of paper together for added strength or for flowers that need different colors on either side of the paper. You can laminate doublette or florist crepe papers with a glue stick or with tacky glue and a flat brush. Always apply the glue thoroughly around the paper, paying special attention to the corners and edges. Make sure the direction of the grain is the same for all layers of paper that you glue together. With these types of paper, you will be able to shape the petal while the glue is still wet and take advantage of the added stretchiness. To laminate more delicate papers, such as fine crepe paper or tissue paper, you can use fusible bonding web or spray adhesive. To laminate sturdy papers like cardstock, use a hot glue gun to apply lines of glue around the edges or center.

Ruffling

Ruffling the edges of your petals will give them a subtle wavy effect. To ruffle your petal, hold the edge of your petal with your thumbs and index fingers and gently pull in opposite directions. Ruffle your petals for flowers like peonies.

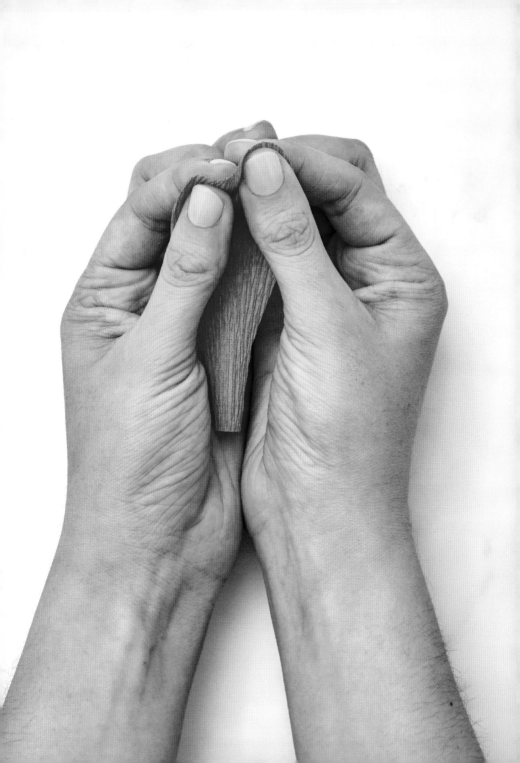

Fringing

A paper fringe is used to simulate the stamens in the flower's center. Cutting a fringe involves making a series of successive cuts along the edge of your paper. Cut a finer and more realistic fringe by carefully making the cuts close together. A wider fringe is used for bolder and more modern designs. To cut a fringe faster, fold your paper cross-wise once or twice and cut multiple layers of paper at once. To cut a uniform fringe, pencil mark or score a horizontal line up to where you want to cut your fringe. To attach your fringe to wire, apply glue along the bottom and wrap it around the top of your wire. Secure with floral tape.

Wiring

Wiring petals consists of adding a straight wire between two layers of paper for added flexibility. Apply glue thoroughly around the paper and place a straight wire vertically down the paper. Sandwich the wire between your two layers of paper. Use a thin floral stem wire that is between 26 and 30 gauge. Wiring petals is great for flowers like the tulip, iris, lily, and magnolia. When making oversize flowers with crepe paper, wire the outer petals for added support. When making wall flowers with crepe paper, wire the upper petals to avoid drooping.

Attaching the Petals

You can glue the petals one by one if you want them placed very precisely, but for a more organic distribution, organize them in clusters. If you attach them as strips or stack them as layers, that will make the project go faster. As you add more petals to your stem, be sure to keep attaching them at the same level on your wire, just below the center/stamens. Otherwise, your flower may move down the wire and it will be very hard to secure it with floral tape.

Wrapping the Stem

The wire becomes the stem as you build the flower on top and wrap it with floral tape or paper strips. You can use floral tape or crepe/tissue paper strips to wrap the wire and to attach leaves to it. Floral tape is easy, as you can just wrap it around the wire, but paper strips will give the project a more finished look. To use paper strips instead of floral tape, cut ¼- to ½-inch (6-mm to 1.3-cm) strips of crepe paper against the grain and stretch them out completely. You can then apply glue along the entire strip, or just apply it every few inches as you wrap it down the wire. You can also use paper strips to create a clean surface if attaching your petals is becoming too slippery. If using plain wire, as opposed to cloth or paper-covered wire, it helps to wrap the wire with floral tape before building your flower. To attach leaves, position them one by one against the wire and secure them with floral tape or by gluing on paper strips.

Coloring Techniques

Painting your paper is another way to add depth and texture to your flowers. You can add finishing touches to your assembled flowers, paint small details on your cut petals, or change the color of your precut paper. Keep in mind that water-based media will wrinkle most papers. Once dry, wrinkles can be fixed by curling them with the edge of your scissors, cupping them with your fingers, or simply smoothing them out between the palms of your hands.

Before you use any of these coloring techniques on a project, it is a good idea to test your coloring techniques on a scrap of paper first and wait to see how the color looks once the paper dries. There's often more than one way to apply each type of coloring method, and some methods work better on certain types of paper than others. Experiment with the coloring techniques that follow to give your paper flowers an artistic touch.

DIP-DYED PAPERS

INKS

ACRYLIC
PAINTS

MARKER

PASTEL

ACRYLIC OR CRAFT PAINT

You can use acrylic or craft paint on papers like cardstock, doublette crepe, florist crepe, and tissue paper. For fine crepe and tissue paper, use the paint sparingly so the paper doesn't rip. Begin by mixing your colors and testing them on paper scraps. Before cutting the paper, you can use a flat brush to make marks up and down your paper, splatter the paint with an old toothbrush, or spray diluted paint on the paper with a spray bottle. After cutting the petals, you can paint fine details with a thin brush. For cardstock, mix the color you want, then with the folded edge of another piece of cardstock pick up the paint and spread a thin layer up and down the paper. Let the paper dry thoroughly before cutting it.

INKS

You can use inks on papers like doublette crepe, florist crepe, fine crepe, and tissue paper. For detailed brush work, use calligraphy inks, alcohol inks, concentrated watercolor, and India or China inks applied with a thin or fan brush and straight out of the jar. If you want to alter the color of your inks, dilute them in rubbing alcohol by adding a few drops of ink into a couple teaspoons of rubbing alcohol until you get the color and saturation you want. For color gradients, brush your paper with water and then apply drops of ink to the wet area. Keep in mind, doublette and florist crepe papers will bleed color when wet. Use this to your advantage and keep the watery pigments that run off the paper to use to color other papers. Alternatively, dilute your inks in approximately ¼ cup (60 ml) rubbing alcohol and pour or brush the color mix directly onto your precut paper. Let dry thoroughly before assembling.

PASTELS AND PANPASTELS

Pastels work well on papers like fine crepe, florist crepe, and doublette crepe. Panpastels have become very popular among paper artists. These are pastels packaged in a pan so they can easily be swiped with a brush or makeup sponge. I recommend applying pastels after assembling a flower to avoid smudging the colors with your fingers while shaping and attaching the petals. Wedge your brush between the stamens and your petals to deposit the pigments and create gradation. Although mostly used as a dry medium, pastels can be mixed with water or rubbing alcohol and applied with a brush for interesting effects. Protect your flowers with a spray fixative after painting them with pastels. Spray your flower evenly from a distance of at least 15 inches (38 cm). This may darken the color slightly. Be careful not to blow on your flowers when working with pastels, as you do not want to breathe in the dust.

MARKERS

Markers are great for cardstock, tissue, fine crepe, and doublette crepe papers. Use a fine-tipped marker to add small details on your cut and shaped petals. Add texture to your petals by drawing lines up and down your paper. To avoid harsh marker lines, start at the base of your petal and feather your marker outward in the direction of the grain. Use a colorless blender to soften any marker streaks if desired. You can also use a broad-tipped marker to lightly dab the edges of your crepe paper petals for a subtle effect. Or use a black permanent marker to draw stamen tips and centers when black crepe paper is not available.

DIP-DYEING

You can dip-dye papers like tissue, fine crepe, florist crepe, and dou-blette crepe. Mix ¼ cup (60 ml) rubbing alcohol with the dye or ink of your choice. You can use liquid fabric dye, food coloring, and even scraps of doublette or florist crepe paper. Control the intensity of the dye by adding more alcohol for a softer color, or less alcohol for more vibrant colors. The paper will absorb the dye very quickly, so you only need to dip it for a couple of seconds. To dye crepe paper, fold each strip several times crosswise and quickly dip one of the edges into your color mix. Let the paper dry before cutting it. To dye tissue paper, cut your tissue paper into strips or squares then gather your paper into bunches and quickly dip one of the edges or corners into the mix. For interesting tie-dye effects, experiment with scrunch-ing or wrinkling your paper. Bleach will also yield interesting results, but mix it only with water (never with alcohol) and use it in a well-ventilated area.

TUTORIALS
FOR
BASIC
FLOWERS

Project No. 1
- - - - - - - - - - - - - -

Cardstock Wall Flower

These cardstock wall flowers are a modern yet whimsical way to decorate your walls for an occasion or long-term. With the help of a hot glue gun, they are easy to craft and can be customized to fit your event's theme or room decor. The recommended paper is cardstock because of its sturdiness. Have fun with the color combinations, and experiment with acrylic paint to give the flower added texture. You can display your flower on the wall with removable hanging strips that hold up to 1 pound. Place the tape of the hanging strips on the back of the flower and on one of the top petals to avoid drooping.

Relevant techniques

cutting, snipping base of petal, laminating, and fringing

Number of petals

16 arranged in 2 layers

Optional coloring / Acrylics

Mix the color you want, then with the folded edge of a piece of cardstock pick up the paint and spread a thin layer up and down your paper. For interesting textures, place two colors next to each other without fully mixing them, pick them up with the folded cardstock, and spread them on the paper. Let the paper dry thoroughly before cutting it.

All dimensions are given as height-by-length.

Materials

Three 8½-by-11-inch (21.5-by-28-cm) sheets of cardstock paper

Color for background petals

Color for foreground petals

Color for the center

Recommended glue:
Hot glue gun

Templates: Wall flower petal

Scissors

Ruler

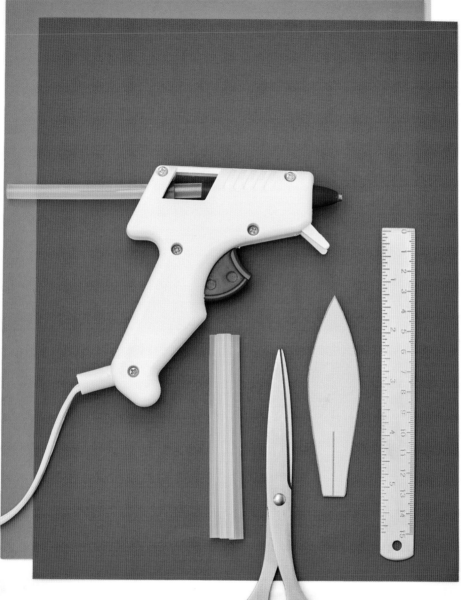

1. Cutting the paper

Cut the background and foreground cardstock into sixteen strips of equal size. Each strip should be approximately 4¼-by-1⅜ inches (11-by-3.5 cm). To do this, cut your paper in half lengthwise and then cut each resulting piece in half crosswise until you get sixteen strips.

2. Cutting the petals

Use the petal template to cut the petals out of your foreground cardstock. Alternatively, cut your own petal design freehand.

3. Laminating the petals

Apply a line of hot glue along a foreground petal and quickly glue it to a background strip. Press and hold briefly.

4. Cutting the outline

Cut the background strip around the foreground petal to create an outline with the background color that's about ⅛-inch (3 mm) thick.

5. Starting to shape the petals

To raise and cup your inner petals, cut a 1¼-inch (3.1-cm) slit at the base of eight petals. Reapply glue to ensure the foreground and the background hold together if needed.

6. Shaping the petals

Apply glue to the bottom of the left flap and overlap it with the bottom of the right flap. Do this with the eight petals where you cut a slit.

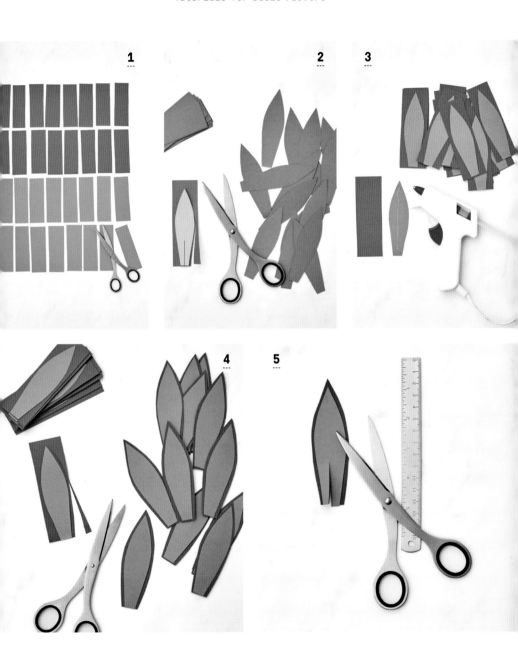

7. Attaching the petals

FIRST LAYER / Cut a 2-by-2-inch (5-by-5-cm) square out of the yellow cardstock. Attach four flat petals on the corners and then fill the gaps with the other four flat petals. Leave enough room in the middle of the square for the flower's center. To glue, apply glue to the back of each petal's base. Press and hold briefly.

8. Attaching the petals

SECOND LAYER / Glue the dimensional petals in between the gaps of your flat petals. Press and hold briefly.

9. Cutting the center

For the center, cut a 3-by-11-inch (7.5-by-28-cm) strip out of the center cardstock and fold it in half lengthwise. Cut a 1-inch-deep (2.5-cm) fringe on the folded edge.

10. Gluing the center

Apply glue along the base (the opposite edge from the fringe) and roll it onto itself to create the center. As you roll, apply more glue as needed.

11. Attaching the center

Apply glue to the back of your center and place it in the middle of your flower. Press and hold briefly. Open your center by fluffing it with your fingers.

Suggested adjustments if using other types of paper

FOR DOUBLETTE CREPE AND FLORIST CREPE / *Petals:* Stretch out your paper and cut out your petal template sixteen times. Make sure the grain of the paper runs parallel to the template arrows. Cut sixteen 4¼-by-1⅜-inch (11-by-3.5-cm) rectangles with the grain running vertically for backing. *Laminate the petals*: With a glue stick or tacky glue, apply glue thoroughly to your petal shapes and attach them to the rectangles and cut around the foreground petal to create an outline with the backing. If you want the second layer of petals to be dimensional, wire them with a 4-inch (10 cm) 26 to 28 gauge wire straight down the middle of each petal. Attach all petals to a 2-by-2-inch (5-by-5-cm) backing with a hot glue gun. CENTER / No change.

7

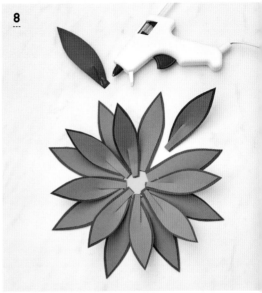

8

9–10

11

Project No. 2
- - - - - - - - - - - - - - - -

Doublette Crepe Paper Tulip

Each of this tulip's six petals is carefully crafted by gluing two layers of paper together. Laminating the petals makes them sturdier and gives them a smooth texture that you can paint with inks. You also have the option of wiring the petals to give them extra mobility, allowing you to open and close your tulip again and again.

Doublette has a different color on each side of the paper. Pick the color that you like, and make sure to glue your paper so that it is the color showing when you fold your petals. The trick to this flower is to thoroughly apply glue when laminating the petals. I prefer to use an extra-strength glue stick for this project, but you can apply tacky glue with the help of a brush or your fingers. If you shape the petals while the glue is still wet, you will be able to create interesting sculptural shapes through cupping and ruffling. To mimic the tulip's thick stem, wrap the wire with extra floral tape.

Relevant techniques

cutting, cupping, ruffling, laminating, wiring, and wrapping the stem

Number of petals

6 arranged in 2 layers

Optional coloring / Inks

You can use concentrated watercolor, calligraphy ink, or India ink. Pick up your paint straight out of the jar using a brush or dilute it with very little rubbing alcohol. Look up tulip photos or botanical illustrations as references to familiarize yourself with the color patterns found in tulips. Use a thin brush to paint delicate brush strokes or a fan brush to paint long brush strokes up and down your petals.

All dimensions are given as height-by-length. The grain of the paper should be running with height.

Materials

Doublette crepe paper (90 g)
    Color for petals
    Green for leaves and stem
    Yellow for center

18 to 20 gauge wire (cut to 9 inches [23 cm])

Recommended glue: Extra-strength glue stick or tacky glue plus a brush to apply

Templates: Tulip petal, Tulip leaf

Scissors

Floral tape

Ruler

Wire cutter

Optional: 26 to 28 gauge wire for wiring petals

1. Center

Cut a 2-by-½-inch (5-by-1.3-cm) rectangle and a ½-by-4-inch (1.3-by-10 cm) strip out of yellow crepe paper. Scrunch and attach your rectangle to the wire with the strip of yellow crepe paper and glue, leaving ¼ inch (6 mm) of the rectangle visible at the top.

2. Stamens

Cut a 2-by-1½-inch (5-by-4-cm) rectangle out of yellow crepe paper. Make four parallel cuts on one of the short sides; each cut approximately 1 inch (2.5 cm) deep and ¼ inch (6 mm) from the next. Twist each resulting tab with your fingers. Apply glue to the base (the short, noncut edge) and wrap it around your stem, approximately 1 inch (2.5 cm) below the top. Secure with floral tape and spread out your stamens evenly around the stem.

3. Laminating the paper

Cut six strips of doublette crepe paper, approximately 3¼-by-4¼ inches (8-by-11 cm) each. Apply glue thoroughly on the right half of one strip (remember, dimensions are given in height by length) and fold it in half to glue the two sides together. Smooth out your paper a little by rubbing it between the palms of your hands. Repeat for all six strips.

Optional: Wire your petals by placing a 4-inch (10-cm) 26 to 28 gauge wire vertically down the middle of your right side and fold the strip in half to glue the two sides together.

4. Cutting the petals

Place your petal template on top of your laminated rectangle and cut around it. Make sure the template arrows match the direction of the grain. Fold the petal's tab back at the base. Repeat for all six petals.

5. Cupping the petals

While the glue is still wet, shape the lower half of your petal. Hold the middle of your petal with your thumbs and index fingers and gently stretch it into a subtle bowl shape. Repeat this motion around the lower half of the petal to get the desired shape. Repeat for all six petals.

6. Ruffling the petals

Ruffle the top of your petal by holding the top edge of the petal with your thumbs and index fingers and gently pulling once in opposite directions to create a wavy effect. Repeat for all petals.

7. Attaching the petals

FIRST LAYER / Apply glue to the folded tab of your first petal and attach it to the stem, just below the stamens. Press and hold briefly. Attach two other petals evenly around the center. Let glue dry and secure with floral tape.

8. Attaching the petals

SECOND LAYER / For the second layer, attach the remaining three petals evenly around the stem, between the gaps of the first layer petals. Attach each petal at the same level on the stem. Secure with floral tape and wrap the tape all the way down the stem.

9. Wrapping the stem

Cut three ½-by-4-inch (1.3-cm-by-10-cm) strips of green crepe paper against the grain. Stretch them out, apply glue, and wrap them down the stem.

10. Cutting the leaves

Cut a 5-by-3-inch (13-by-7.5-cm) rectangle of green doublette crepe paper. Fold it in half along the grain and cut out the leaf template for a total of two leaves. Curl your leaves slightly.

11. Attaching the leaves

Scrunch the base of your first leaf and place approximately 4 inches (10 cm) below the flower, then secure it to the stem with a crepe paper strip and glue. Place your second leaf ½ inch (1.3 cm) below the first leaf and secure it with a crepe paper strip that you will then wrap all the way down the stem.

Suggested adjustments if using other types of paper

FOR FLORIST CREPE PAPER / *Center, stamens, stem, leaves:* no change. *Petals:* Stretch your paper before cutting and laminating. Cut and shape your petals while the glue is still wet.

FOR FINE CREPE PAPER / *Center, stamens, stem, leaves:* no change. *Petals*: Be careful not to rip the paper while applying glue.

Project No. 3

Florist Crepe Paper Open Peony

Peonies are one of the most popular flowers to re-create in paper, because their fluffiness makes them the perfect focal flower for bouquets and arrangements. This paper peony explores the cupping technique, and the recommended paper is florist crepe because of its stretch. The trick to this peony is to repeat the cupping motion up and down the petal to get an elongated shape. Once you finish assembling the flower, it is important that you fluff the center and bring down the petals for a more organic look.

Relevant techniques

cutting, cupping, ruffling, fringing, attaching petals, and wrapping the stem

Number of petals

15 arranged in 3 layers

Optional coloring / Panpastels

Apply pastels with a brush as a finishing touch, once the peony is completely assembled. Begin by mixing the color you want and pick it up with your brush. Wedge your brush between the base of your petals and the stamens to deposit the pastels. Although mostly used as a dry medium, pastels can be mixed with water or alcohol and applied with a brush for interesting effects.

All dimensions are given as height-by-length. The grain of the paper should be running with height.

Materials

Florist crepe paper (180 g)

Color for the petals

Green for the leaves

Yellow for the center

Pink scraps for carpels

18 to 20 gauge wire (cut to 9 inches [23 cm])

Recommended glue: Extra-strength glue stick

Templates: Peony petal, Peony calyx / leaf

Scissors

Floral tape

Ruler

Wire cutter

1. Carpels

Cut three 2-by-½-inch (5-by-1.3-cm) pieces of pink crepe paper. Wrap each piece with floral tape, leaving ¼ inch (6 mm) of pink paper visible at the top. Attach the bottom halves of the three carpels together to the top of your wire with floral tape and wrap it all the way down the stem.

2. Stamens

Cut a 2½-by-10-inch (6.5-by-25-cm) strip of yellow crepe and stretch it out completely. Cut a 1½-inch (4-cm) fringe on one of the long sides of the strip. Apply glue along the base (the opposite edge from the fringe) and wrap the fringe around the stem, approximately ¾ inch (2 cm) from the top of the carpels. Secure with floral tape.

3. Cutting the petals

Cut a 4-by-3-inch (10-by-7.5-cm) rectangle in the color of your petals. Fold it in half along the grain and cut around your petal template, which will create two petals. You will need eight rectangles to make a total of fifteen petals. Once your petals are cut out, fold back the base of each petal into a ⅓-inch (8-mm) tab.

4. Shaping the petals

CUPPING / To cup your petals, place your thumbs and index fingers approximately 1 inch (2.5 cm) below the upper edge. Stretch your petal to create a subtle rounded shape. Move your fingers down ½ inch (1.3 cm) and stretch again. Do this two more times, until you reach the folded tab. Repeating the cupping motion up and down the petal will result in an elongated cupped shape. Smooth out any wrinkles. Repeat for all fifteen petals.

5. Shaping the petals

RUFFLING / Ruffle the edge of your petal by placing your fingers on the upper edge and gently pulling the paper once in opposite directions to create a subtle wave effect. Repeat for all fifteen petals.

6. Attaching the petals

FIRST LAYER / Apply glue to the folded tab of your first petal and attach it right under the stamens. The cupped side of the petal should be facing up. For your first layer, attach four other petals evenly around the stem. Press and hold briefly.

7. Attaching the petals

SECOND AND THIRD LAYERS / For the second layer, attach five more petals between the gaps of the first five petals. It is important that you attach each petal at the same level on the stem, instead of progressively lower down the stem. For the third layer, attach the remaining five petals, filling in the gaps of the previous layers. Secure with floral tape between layers if it's becoming slippery and the petals aren't staying in place.

8. Cutting the calyx / leaves

Cut three 4-by-2-inch (10-by-5-cm) rectangles out of green crepe paper and stretch them out completely. Fold each rectangle in half along the grain twice and cut out your calyx/leaf template. This will create four pieces. Repeat for a total of twelve pieces.

CALYX / For the calyx, curl the upper half of five of the green pieces. Apply glue below the dotted line and attach them evenly around the stem. The long tab should be hugging the stem and connecting the bulk of the petal bases to the stem. The curled part should be right under your petals.

9. Wrapping the stem

Cut a ½-by-4-inch (1.3-by-10-cm) strip of green crepe paper against the grain and stretch it out completely. Apply glue and wrap it around the stem to secure the calyx and petals.

10. Leaves

Stack three leaves (from step 8), twist their bases together, and fan them out. Repeat with a second group of three leaves. Attach the base of the first group approximately 3 inches (7.5 cm) below your flower. Secure with a strip of green crepe paper and glue. Attach the base of a second group of three leaves approximately 4 inches (10 cm) below your flower (you will have one leftover calyx/leaf piece). Secure with a strip of green crepe paper that you will then wrap all the way down the stem.

Suggested adjustments if using other types of paper

FOR DOUBLETTE CREPE / *Carpels, stamens, calyx, stem, leaves*: no change. *Petals*: Add more petals if you notice any gaps after assembly.

FOR FINE CREPE / *Carpels, stamens, stem:* no change. *Calyx, leaves:* Cut three 4-by-4-inch (10-by-10-cm) pieces out of green crepe paper. Do not stretch out the paper before cutting. *Petals:* Cut a total of twenty-eight petals. Scrunch the base of each petal before attaching it to the stem. Attach the petals in four layers of seven petals each.

9

10

Project No. 4

Fine Crepe Paper Butterfly Ranunculus

To create this butterfly ranunculus, you will need to attach the petals in clusters. This makes it easy to evenly and organically space out the petals without leaving noticeable gaps. The recommended paper is fine crepe paper because of its subtle stretch and delicate texture. The calyx of a butterfly ranunculus adds a nice finishing touch, but you can skip this step depending on how you will display the flower. The same goes for the leaves. Fluff your flower and bring down your petals when finished assembling.

Relevant techniques
cutting, cupping, fringing,
attaching petals, and wrapping
the stem

Number of petals
26 arranged in 3 layers

Optional coloring /
Paint markers
Paint your petals right after
cutting them but before shaping
them. Stack them in groups of
four and then dab the edges of
your petals with your marker's tip
and allow the paper to absorb the
ink. You can also use your marker
to paint vertical streaks up and
down your paper before cutting
the petals. Paint the streaks in
the direction of the grain.

All dimensions are given
as height-by-length. The
grain of the paper should be
running with height.

Materials

Fine crepe paper (60 g)
   Color for the petals
   Black for the center
   Green for the leaves

18 to 20 gauge floral wire (cut to
9 inches [23 cm])

Recommended glue:
Extra-strength glue stick
or tacky glue and a brush to
apply it

Templates: Butterfly
ranunculus petal,
butterfly ranunculus calyx,
butterfly ranunculus leaf

Scissors

Floral tape

Ruler

Wire cutter

1. Center

Cut two 1½-by-1½-inch (4-by-4-cm) squares of black crepe paper. Crumple one square into a little ball and place it on top of your wire. Cover it with the other square and secure with floral tape.

2. Stamens

Cut a 2-by-5-inch (5-by-13-cm) strip of black paper, stretch it out, and fold it in half lengthwise. Cut a ¼-inch (6-mm) fringe on the folded edge. Apply glue along the bottom edge opposite the fringe and wrap it evenly around your center, aligning it with the top of the little ball. Secure with floral tape and wrap the tape all the way down the wire.

3. Cutting the petals

Cut a 2-by-5-inch (5-by-13-cm) strip of fine crepe paper in the color of your petals. Fold your strip in half two times crosswise and cut around the template to create four petals. You will need a total of seven strips to create the twenty-six petals needed.

4. Shaping the petals

CUPPING / Keep the petals stacked together to shape them and cup four petals at once. To do this, place your thumbs in the middle of your petals and stretch gently from the center outward to create a bowl shape.

5. Assembling the petals

FOUR-PETAL CLUSTERS / With the cupped sides facing up, group four petals together and then fan them apart so that each petal overlaps approximately half of the petal next to it. Glue them together at their bases as shown. Assemble a total of two clusters of four petals each.

6. Assembling the petals

THREE-PETAL CLUSTERS / With the cupped sides facing up, group three petals together by placing two petals next to each other and then placing one petal on top, where the two petals meet. Glue them together at their bases as shown. Assemble a total of six clusters of three petals each.

7. Attaching the petals

FIRST LAYER / With the cupped sides facing up, attach the first four-petal cluster to the stem, just below the stamens. Attach the second four-petal cluster right across your first cluster. Press and hold briefly.

8. Attaching the petals

SECOND LAYER / With the cupped sides facing *down*, attach three of your three-petal clusters evenly around the stem. Make sure each petal cluster is on the same level as the previous layer, just below the stamens.

5

6

7

8–9

9. Attaching the petals

THIRD LAYER / With the cupped sides facing *down*, attach your remaining three three-petal clusters evenly around the stem. Let glue dry and then secure with floral tape.

10. Optional

CALYX / Cut a 1½-by-3-inch (4-by-7.5-cm) strip of green crepe paper. Accordion-fold it into five equal parts and cut out the calyx template. Curl all five pieces above the dotted line. Apply glue below the dotted line and attach them evenly around the stem right below the petals. Cut two ½-by-4-inch (1.3-by-10-cm) strips of green crepe paper, apply glue, and wrap them down the stem.

11. Leaves

Cut a 3-by-4½-inch (7.5-by-11.5-cm) rectangle of green crepe paper and accordion-fold it along the grain into three equal parts. Cut a total of three leaves using your leaf template. Cut two ½-by-4-inch (1.3-by-10-cm) strips of green crepe paper. Scrunch and twist the base of each leaf and attach them to the stem approximately 3 to 4 inches (7.5 to 10 cm) below the flower using a paper strip and glue.

Suggested adjustments if using other types of paper

FOR FLORIST CREPE / *Center, stamens, calyx:* Stretch out your paper completely before cutting. *Petals:* Cut six 2-by-3-inch (5-by-7.5-cm) strips. With the help of your ruler, gently stretch them a little until they measure approximately 2-by-4½ inches (5-by-11.5 cm). Fold the strips twice along the grain and cut out your petal template. Shape, cluster, and attach your petals as per the tutorial. *Leaves:* Stretch out your paper completely and cut three leaf shapes. Twist the base on each leaf and attach to the stem.

FOR DOUBLETTE CREPE / *Center, stamens, calyx:* Stretch out the paper completely before cutting. *Petals:* Make sure the same color of the paper is always facing up. *Leaves:* Stretch out your paper completely and cut three leaf shapes. Twist base on each and attach to the stem.

10 **11**

Project No. 5
- - - - - - - - - - - - - - - -

Tissue Paper Dahlia

This tissue paper dahlia is easy to put together and can even be made out of upcycled tissue paper. Dahlias usually have many petals and can be time-consuming to complete, but this technique allows you to simulate the dahlia's petals without having to attach each one individually. It also uses the same template for your petals, center, and leaves, and you even shape them the same way. You will need enough paper to cut eleven squares, each one measuring 5-by-5 inches (13-by-13 cm). The recommended coloring technique is dip-dyeing the paper after cutting out the template shape. Once finished, fluff your petals with your fingers and bring down the flat petals slightly.

Relevant techniques

cutting, scrunching, attaching petals, and wrapping the stem

Number of petals

8 arranged in 5 layers

Optional coloring /
Dip-dyeing

You can make the mix to dip-dye your paper by mixing food coloring with rubbing alcohol or mixing bleach with water. Test your color mix on paper scraps before applying it to your petals. Color the edges of your petals by dip-dyeing the folded petals right after cutting out the template shapes. Hold your folded petals by the pointy corner and dip them into your color mix to color the petal edges. Conversely, hold your folded petals by the petal edges to color the center. Dip for a few seconds and hang to dry. Wait for the paper to dry completely before unfolding the petals.

All dimensions are given as
height-by-length.

Materials

Tissue paper

Color for center

Color for petals

Color for leaves and stem

18 to 20 gauge wire (cut to 9 inches [23 cm])

Recommended glue:
Extra-strength glue stick, tacky glue with a brush to apply it, or hot glue gun

Templates: Dahlia petal / center / leaf

Scissors

Floral tape

Ruler

Wire cutter

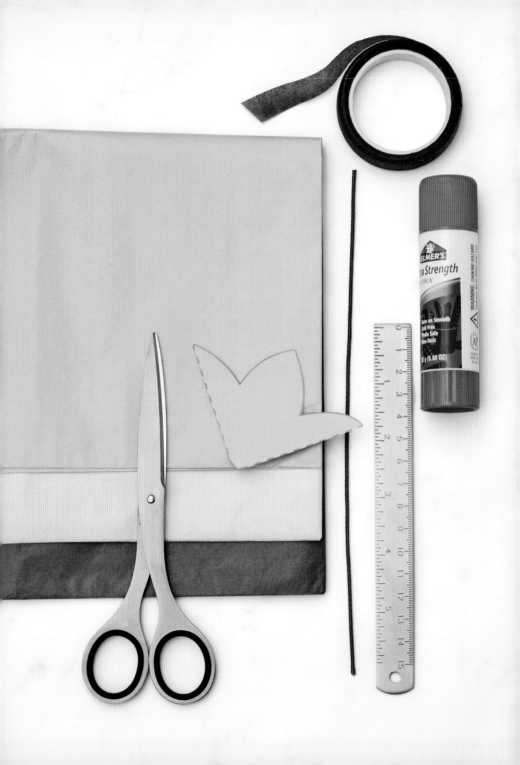

1. Cutting the paper

Cut eleven 5-by-5-inch (13-by-13-cm) squares of tissue paper, eight in the color of your petals, two in the color of your leaves, and one in the color of your center. Cut three ½-by-4-inch (1.3-by-10-cm) strips in the color of your stem.

2. Cutting the petals, center, and leaves

Stack five single squares of any color, since all the parts of the dahlia are cut and shaped the same way. Fold the group in half lengthwise and then crosswise to get a 2½-by-2½-inch (6.5-by-6.5-cm) folded square. Place your template on top of your folded square by aligning the template's corner with the folded squares' closed corner. Cut around the template's solid lines but not around the dotted lines. Repeat for all squares.

3. Corners

Cut off a tiny bit of the corner of each group and separate them so you have eight petals, one center, and two leaves.

4. Shaping

To shape, place one finger in the center and scrunch the paper around it on the other side to create a ½-inch (1.3-cm) base. Do this with four groups of petals, one center, and two leaves. Leave four groups of petals flat.

5. Center

Apply glue to the base of your shaped center and attach it to the top of your wire. Secure with floral tape and wrap it all the way down the wire.

6. Attaching the shaped petals

One by one, apply glue to the base of the four shaped petals and attach them evenly around the center. Secure with floral tape.

7. Attaching the flat petals

Apply glue around the center of your flat petals. One by one, insert the wire through the center of each flat petal and push them up to glue them to the bottom of the shaped petals. Make sure to rotate each flat petal slightly before gluing it to the base of the flower. Press and hold briefly between petals. Insert all four flat petals or create more if you want a fuller flower.

8. Wrapping the stem

Once your flat petals are securely attached, cover your stem with strips of tissue paper in the color of your leaves.

9. Leaves

Apply glue to the base of your shaped leaves and attach them to the stem, approximately 4 inches (10 cm) below your flower. Secure them with strips of tissue paper and glue. Wrap them all the way down the stem.

Suggested adjustments if using other types of paper

FOR FLORIST CREPE, DOUBLETTE CREPE, FINE CREPE / *Petals, center, and leaves*: Cut your 5-by-5-inch (13-by-13-cm) squares and stretch them out completely. Fold each square in half twice, first along the grain and then against the grain. Cut out your petals, center, and leaves from one folded piece of paper one at a time.

BEYOND FLOWERS

There are many applications for your finished paper flowers. I've given them away as gifts to friends and family and made a host of fun projects, from wedding bouquets and centerpieces to event decorations, party favors, floral crowns, and miniature pins. Below are some quick project ideas that are brought to life by paper flowers. You can complete these projects using the paper flowers in this book.

Bouquets
and
Arrangements

PAPER FLOWER BOUQUET
WITH FRESH FOLIAGE

Paper flowers make great bouquets because you don't have to worry if the flowers are in season together, they don't need water, and they will last forever. When creating a bouquet, choose flowers that show a variety of textures, shapes, and sizes. You can use the stemmed flowers in this book as a bouquet recipe. To create color harmony, craft your flowers in an analogous color palette, or in varying shades of one color. Use the peonies as focal blooms, painted tulips as touches of bold color, butterfly ranunculus for texture, and dahlias to add volume. For a luscious bouquet, mix your flowers with real foliage, like seeded eucalyptus and lemon leaf. Gather your focal flowers in a bunch and arrange the foliage around them. Make sure it does not overshadow or hide your flowers. Keep adding smaller flowers to fill in any gaps. Try not to push the flower heads together; instead have them at different levels to add depth and dimension. Once you've got a bouquet shape you like, wrap floral tape several times around your stems. Then use a wire cutter to cut your stems to the desired length. Finish your bouquet by covering the floral tape with ribbon.

TULIP ARRANGEMENT

For a tulip arrangement, pick a vase that is more than half as tall as your tulip stems. A vintage milk bottle, a bud vase, or a cylinder vase will all work well. Build five to six paper tulips on stems, and for each flower, cut two oversize leaf shapes out of an entire 10-by-4-inch (25-by-10-cm) sheet of green doublette crepe, folded in half along the grain. You can laminate the leaves for added mobility and sturdiness. Twist the base and attach two leaves to each tulip. Spread out your tulips in various directions. Curve and bend the stems for a more natural look. If you wired the petals, you can open and close the flower heads to varying degrees.

Gifts

ARTFULLY WRAPPED SINGLE FLOWER

A handmade paper flower artfully wrapped in tissue paper is a thoughtful gift idea for birthdays, anniversaries, and graduations. You can gift a carefully crafted single stem on special occasions like Valentine's Day and Mother's Day. Paper is also the traditional material to celebrate first wedding anniversaries. To wrap your paper flower, begin by picking a paper color that matches or complements your flower. Black tissue paper or kraft paper will match any flower.

WITH TISSUE PAPER

Cut out one rectangle of 8½-by-11-inch (21.5-by-28-cm) black tissue paper and one of white. Stack the two sheets and rotate 45 degrees, then fold the left corners in. Place your flower in the middle and fold your right corners in. Gather and scrunch your paper around the stem approximately 4 inches (10 cm) below your flower head and wrap with floral tape. Finish the presentation by tying with a piece of ribbon.

WITH A CARDSTOCK CONE

Roll one 8½-by-11-inch (21.5-by-28-cm) sheet of cardstock into an elongated cone. Tape the bottom of the cone as well as the edges where the paper meets on the inside and outside. Insert your flower and matching tissue paper into the cone.

ARTFULLY WRAPPED SINGLE FLOWER *page 114*

Decorations and Events

WALL FLOWER BACKDROP

Make a paper flower backdrop with cardstock wall flowers for your next event. Cardstock is a popular choice for events because of its sturdiness. It comes in a wide range of colors that can be customized to the event's theme and color palette. To add texture and depth, paint the cardstock with acrylics before cutting it. Play with the scale of the flowers by changing the size of your templates to fit an entire sheet of cardstock. Focus on a few oversize flowers and arrange other flowers in a variety of sizes around them. Vary the petal shape from pointy to rounded on some of your flowers and cut the edges of your petals with decorative scissors for interesting effects. Attach your finished flowers to the wall with the help of removable hanging strips that hold up to one pound. If you have enough wall flowers, you can even treat them as party favors and invite guests to take them home with them at the end of the event.

BUTTERFLY RANUNCULUS FLORAL CROWN

Make a delicate butterfly ranunculus flower crown for a themed party or a bridal shower. Begin by wrapping two 22 gauge wires around your head to measure its circumference. Twist the ends of the wires together to form the base of your floral crown. For the flowers, make five to six butterfly ranunculus, assembled on 22 gauge wire stems cut to 5 inches (13 cm). You can skip the calyx, but attach two or three leaves just 1 inch (2.5 cm) below the flower head. To begin assembling the floral crown, place your first butterfly ranunculus against the base and twist the stem around it directly under the leaves. Place your second butterfly ranunculus and twist the stem around the base in the same direction. Continue attaching the rest of your butterfly ranunculus until half of your base is covered or attach three on one side of your face and two on the other. Cover the rest of your base with floral tape or crepe paper strips for a more polished look.

TEMPLATES

All dimensions are given as height-by-length.
The grain of the paper should be running with height, up and down
the longest part of your petal, leaf, or calyx. Cut
along solid lines and fold or scrunch along dotted lines.

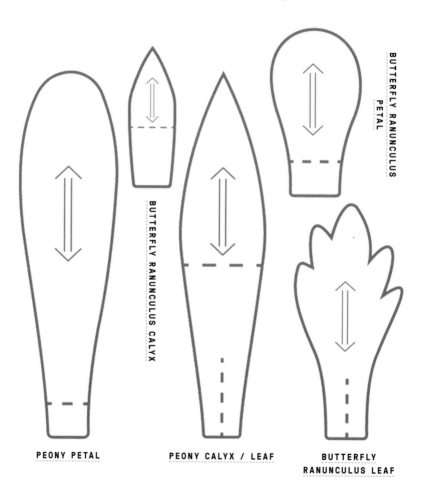

BUTTERFLY RANUNCULUS
PETAL

BUTTERFLY RANUNCULUS CALYX

PEONY PETAL

PEONY CALYX / LEAF

BUTTERFLY
RANUNCULUS LEAF

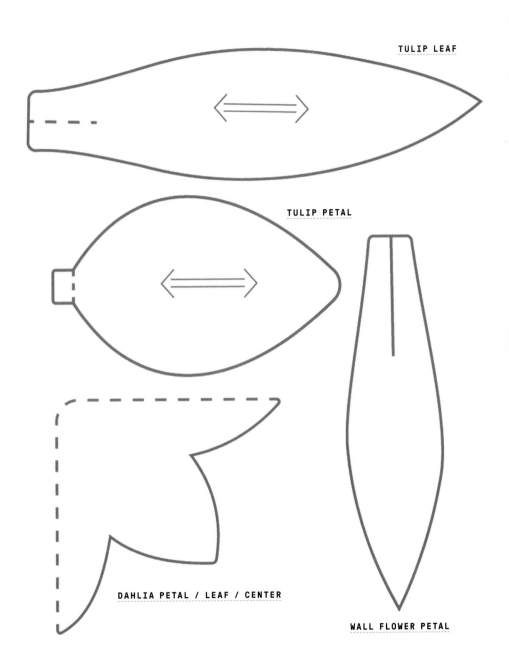

TULIP LEAF

TULIP PETAL

DAHLIA PETAL / LEAF / CENTER

WALL FLOWER PETAL

GLOSSARY

Accordion-fold: Series of alternating folds to create sections of similar size

Cardstock paper: Thick, durable paper in solid colors

Cupping: Shaping paper into a rounded shape

Curling: Shaping paper into a curved or rolled shape

Decorative scissors: Scissors with special edge designs

Dip-dyeing: Dipping your paper into dyes such as food coloring, bleach, or ink

Doublette crepe paper: Smooth crepe paper with good stretch

Fine crepe paper: Delicate crepe paper with subtle stretch

Floral stem wire: Flexible aluminum wire sometimes covered in cloth or paper

Floral tape: Stretchable tape that adheres only to itself

Florist crepe paper: Textured crepe paper with plenty of stretch

Focal flowers: Large flowers that draw the attention of the viewer

Freehand cutting: Cutting petals without the aid of a template

Fringing: Making successive cuts along the edge of the paper

Fusible bonding web: Thin layer of fiber that bonds two pieces of paper together when ironed. Generally used to bond layers of fabric together.

Gauge: Measures the thickness of wire

Glue stick: Solid glue in a push-up tube

Grain of the paper: Vertical ridges that give crepe paper its stretchiness

Hot glue gun: Precision gun to dispense hot melted glue

Laminating: Gluing two pieces of paper together

Mod Podge: Glue, sealer, and finish in one for all types of paper

Panpastels: Chalk pastels in a pan format

Ruffling: Shaping the edge of the petal into a subtle curve

Scrunching: Gathering paper sections with your fingers

Spray fixative: Spray adhesive used to preserve paint and protect finished flowers

Tacky glue: All-purpose glue with thick consistency

Template: Guide to cut petal flower shapes

Tissue paper: Lightweight paper used mainly for gift wrapping

Twisting: Rolling a piece of paper between your fingers

Wiring: Inserting a piece of thin floral wire between two papers

RESOURCES

I hope that this quick introduction to paper flower crafting will excite you into further exploring the craft. If you want to learn more about the world of contemporary paper flowers, there are many fantastic books on paper flowers out there, such as *The Exquisite Book of Paper Flowers* by Livia Cetti.

You can find the following papers and materials at these brick-and-mortar stores:

Blick Art Materials: florist crepe paper 180 g, doublette crepe paper 90 g, fine crepe paper 60 g, tissue paper, cardstock paper, floral tape, floral stem wire, coloring supplies, all types of adhesives.

Michaels: cardstock paper, tissue paper, floral tape, floral stem wire, coloring supplies, all types of adhesives.

You can find the following papers and materials online at:

Shopliagriffith.com: florist crepe paper (called heavy floristic crepe), doublette crepe paper 90 g, fine crepe paper 60 g, tissue paper, floral tape, floral stem wire, coloring supplies.

Cartefini.com: florist crepe paper 180 g, fine crepe paper 60 g.

Paperflowersupplies.com: doublette crepe paper, florist crepe paper 180 g, fine crepe paper 32 g, floral stem wire, floral tape, coloring supplies.

Papermart: florist crepe paper 100 g and 180 g, tissue paper, floral stem wire, floral tape, fine crepe paper 28 g.

Rosemille.com: doublette crepe, fine crepe 32 g, floral stem wire, floral tape.

Amazon.com: florist crepe paper 100 to 180 g, doublette crepe paper 90 g, fine crepe paper 32 to 60 g, tissue paper, cardstock paper, floral tape, floral stem wire, coloring supplies, all types of adhesives.

A variety of tutorials and templates for different types of paper can be found at www.liagriffith.com.

Take video lessons on Skillshare, Teachable, CreativeLive, and Bluprint.

Join the paper florist community on social media by searching for @thepaperfloristsorg on Instagram and The Paper Florists on Facebook.

Look for workshops in your area taught by local paper flower artists.

Acknowledgments

To **Matilde**, **Magic**, and **Jochi**, thank you for your love and support.

To **Abigail Peterson**, **Angela Liguori**, **Andrea Reyes**, **Jessie Chui**, and **Stacey Lee**, thank you for your help and enthusiasm.

To the **paper florist community** on Instagram and Facebook, thank you for your creativity and inspiration.